Yellowstone

A Unique Ecosystem

Written by Jenny Feely
Series Consultant: Linda Hoyt

WorldWise™
Content-based Learning

Contents

Introduction

An active volcano bubbles away under the ground, creating geysers that shoot water a hundred metres into the air. Mud pools boil and clouds of steam hiss from cracks and holes in the ground called fumaroles.

Over millions of years, rivers and **glaciers** have carved the landscape and filled lakes with mineral-rich, life-giving water.

Yellowstone National Park in the United States is a place of unforgettable beauty and astonishing natural features. Situated on a high **plateau** surrounded by mountain ranges, its valleys and wetlands are the perfect place for plants and animals to thrive.

It is a place of varied and abundant life. With its huge forests, grassy meadows and vast wetlands, it is home to herds of elk and bison. It is a place where wolves and bears roam free.

As well, Yellowstone National Park is a place people love to visit. They come to see the natural wonders, to camp and hike, to take photographs and to marvel at the many and varied plants and animals they see.

In 1871, the US government surveyed this region, and its great natural beauty was painted and photographed. In 1872, a law declared Yellowstone a national park, the first in the United States. Yellowstone National Park became a protected area, a place where laws protect the plants and animals that live there.

Chapter 1

Getting to know Yellowstone

The last wild place?

As people drive into Yellowstone National Park, they may pass under the arch that reads "For the Benefit and Enjoyment of the People".

But that is not the whole story.

Yellowstone National Park is there for the benefit of all the living things that exist in the park.

Greater Yellowstone is described by scientists as a unique ecosystem – a single tract of about nine million hectares of land – that provides scientists with the opportunity to study the **interdependence** of plants and animals in their natural habitat. This interdependence is strengthened by the landscape – mountains, **alpine** meadows, valleys, canyons, waterfalls, lakes and hot springs. It is one of the largest patches of **pristine** wild land in the United States, and it is one of the last relatively unspoiled **temperate** climate ecosystems on Earth.

It is there to teach us how nature works.

Yellowstone:
An amazing ecosystem

Yellowstone, like all ecosystems, is a place where a range of living things interact with each other and their surroundings to form a community.

Within this huge, interdependent ecosystem are smaller, different habitats. The presence of so many different habitats in Yellowstone is the reason there is such a diverse range of plants and animals living there.

These habitats range in temperature, from the steaming **super-heated** pools to the ice-covered mountain tops. The amount of rainfall and available water in each habitat can also vary widely.

But, whatever the conditions, the plants and animals that live in the park have the **adaptations** needed to find food, water and shelter there, living healthy lives,and reproducing each year.

Most importantly, in each habitat in Yellowstone there is a balance between the plants and animals that live there.

All these things make Yellowstone a huge, thriving, healthy ecosystem.

Types of habitats

Yellowstone has a range of land-based habitats. Around 80 per cent of the park is covered in forest. There are also areas with low-growing shrubs and grasses called sagebrush steppe, and wildflower-strewn alpine meadows. The grasses and other plants of the steppes provide food for wandering herds of elk and bison. These animals are hunted by wolves.

There is also a range of water-based habitats in Yellowstone. These include Yellowstone Lake, hot thermal pools, rivers and ponds. They support a huge number of living things including fish, waterbirds, frogs, beavers and river otters, as well as large numbers of water plants. Yellowstone Lake is an important habitat for the Yellowstone cut-throat trout that spawns in the late spring and early summer. These fish are an important food source for many birds as well as bears, river otters and mink.

Find out more

There are 67 species of mammals and 285 species of birds in Yellowstone. Find out about other types of living things in Yellowstone.

A herd of bison grazing in Yellowstone.

9

Why is Yellowstone so diverse?

Yellowstone National Park has so many interesting and different habitats because of the varied terrain in the parks where mountains, valleys and even deep canyons can be found.

Different plants and animals are found in different parts of the park. This is because of the varying kinds of soil that are found in each place. Lodgepole pine forests grow where the soil is poorest. Meadows and wide lush grasslands flourish in the places where the soil is richer, providing food for many animals.

Importantly, the national park is so diverse because each area is protected from being changed by people. This means the land flourishes and, with it, the animals that live there.

Deer

Pronghorn antelope

Bison

Grizzly bear

The grasslands support huge herds of elk, bison and deer – animals that need to be able to graze across large areas to stay healthy. As well, these areas provide protected corridors for animals that migrate from place to place as the seasons change. For pronghorn antelope and bison, this is important, enabling them to have enough seasonal food and to give birth in warmer conditions.

Large predators such as grizzly bears and wolves also benefit from the protection in the park. The existence of the herds of herbivores provides food for these hunters. People are not allowed to hunt in the park and this protects the wolves and bears. Without national parks such as Yellowstone, it is likely that grizzly bears and wolves would not survive in much of the United States.

Living in Yellowstone

All living things in Yellowstone depend on the sun above and the ground below to sustain life. They all need water. As well, the plants and animals depend on each other for survival.

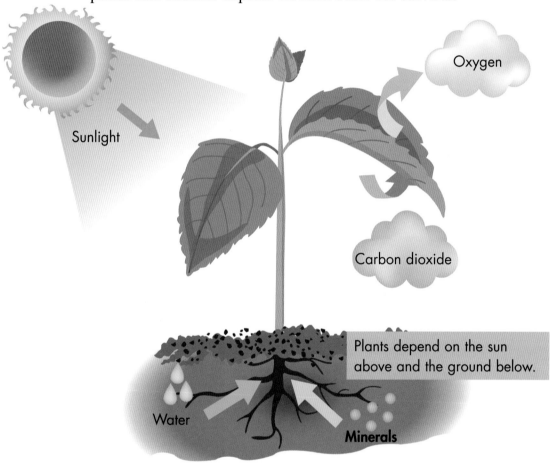

Sunlight

Oxygen

Carbon dioxide

Plants depend on the sun above and the ground below.

Water

Minerals

Life-giving sunshine

The light and energy from the sun are vital for the abundant life in Yellowstone. Plants, such as the trees that grow in the forest and the grasses that grow in the meadows, absorb light from the sun and turn it into food. Sunlight enables plants to grow leaves and flowers and to develop seeds from which new plants will grow.

Fertile soil

The soil in Yellowstone is also important for plants that use their roots to take up the nutrients they need from the dirt they grow in. Yellowstone's soil is very fertile because it was formed by volcanic eruptions thousands of years ago. Mineral-rich ash was dropped on the land.

Abundant water

Life in Yellowstone also flourishes because the park receives a higher level of rain and snow than surrounding areas. This is due to the shape of the surrounding mountains that funnel storms and clouds into the park. Having a large amount of water available means that Yellowstone has many ponds, lakes and even underwater **thermal vents**.

As the rainwater runs off and filters through the soil, it picks up minerals and other nutrients from the rich volcanic soil. Plants use the minerals in the soil and the water that flows freely through the park to grow and thrive.

13

From plants to animals

Plant-eating animals such as elk, moose, squirrels and rabbits get the nutrition and energy they need from the plants they eat.

The energy and nutrients stored in the plant's leaves, stems, bark, flowers and seeds pass into the animals when they eat the plants.

From animal to animal

Animals such as wolves, coyotes, mountain lions and hawks take in the energy and nutrients they need when they eat the plant-eating animals. Animals such as bears eat both plants and animals to get the nutrition they need.

Yellowstone food cycle

Back to the earth

Yellowstone's plants and animals also return nutrients to the ground. Plants do this when they drop their leaves or die. As the leaves, stems and bark rot, the nutrients in them return to the soil.

Animals do this as their droppings rot into the soil and when their bodies decompose after they die, returning nutrients for new plants to take up as the cycle continues.

Chapter 3

Surviving the threat of extinction

A grizzly problem

Once, thousands of grizzly bears roamed freely throughout the Yellowstone area. The establishment of the national park provided a safe place where grizzly bears were protected and able to thrive. But in the 1870s, poachers continued to hunt the bears even inside the park boundaries.

As Yellowstone became a famous place where people could watch and feed grizzly bears "in the wild", interactions between visitors and the bears caused harm to the bears and to humans. Bears became familiar with people, and they were attracted to the food they brought to the park. There was an increase in incidents where bears damaged property or hurt people in their search for food. Park rangers, who look after the welfare of the bears, relocated those bears that had caused problems. And sometimes they had to kill the bears to protect people.

The number of bears in the park plummeted, and by the 1960s it was thought that there were fewer than 250 bears left in the park. By the 1970s, the Yellowstone grizzly bear had become an **endangered** animal.

A healthy grizzly population

To protect the bears, new policies banned people from feeding and interacting with them. Open rubbish dumps were no longer allowed in the park, and bear-proof rubbish bins were installed. All visitors to the park had to store their food out of the reach of bears. The grizzly bears were now forced to find their food in the wild. Rangers worked to ensure that important food for bears, such as white bark pine and cut-throat trout, was well managed. The return of the grey wolf to Yellowstone meant that the bears have access to more food. The bears eat dead animals that the wolves have killed.

Today, there is a healthy grizzly population, with more than 750 grizzly bears in Yellowstone. The bear has been removed from the endangered species list. But ensuring that the grizzly bear continues to thrive and survive in Yellowstone remains an ongoing challenge for the rangers.

Did you know?
Bears are omnivores. This means that they eat both plants and animals.

▲ Cars stop to allow a grizzly bear to cross the road in Yellowstone.

17

The return of the wolves

In the past, people thought Yellowstone would be a better place without wolves. But they were wrong. Grey wolves are essential to the health and well-being of the animals and plants that live there.

What caused the wolves to disappear?

Almost from the time that Yellowstone National Park was established, and cattle ranchers and sheep grazers moved into the area, wolves were hunted. People feared them and did not want them to eat their sheep and cattle. Eventually, all of the wolves in the park were killed.

But this created unexpected problems in the national park. Grey wolves sit at the top of the food chain. They are fierce and relentless predators that hunt elk and other animals that live in the park. Without wolves, there was an overpopulation of elk in the park, and this degraded the tree and vegetation growth, which meant less food for other herbivores and caused **erosion**.

Why were the wolves returned?

In the 1990s, after 70 years of absence, grey wolves were brought back to Yellowstone. This was done to reduce the number of elk that lived in the park. Rangers kept a close eye on the wolves. They wanted to measure the effect of the wolves on the elk herds, which had reached sizes greater than 20,000.

What effect did the return of the wolves have?

The wolves quickly established hunting territories where they hunted elk. The wolves killed some elk, but not enough to reduce the herd sizes by much.

Elk eat plants – in particular, young trees such as willow and larch. Previously, the elk herds had no need to keep moving, and they stayed in the same place until all the food was used up. This led to overgrazing, where plants are eaten too quickly for them to **regenerate**. Overgrazing had wiped out a lot of the trees that grew along the banks of Yellowstone's rivers. The roots of these trees were important for keeping the banks of the rivers intact and preventing the water in the river from washing the soil away.

Without the trees, the rivers were washing away the fertile soil in their banks, leading to fewer trees. But the presence of the wolves changed the behaviour of the elk. The wolves kept the elk moving from place to place and prevented overgrazing. The trees began to return, and the erosion of the riverbanks stopped.

Perhaps a surprising result of the return of the wolves was that the health of the elk improved, too. With fewer elk, there was enough food to go around. With the elk moving more often, there was more food, too.

 Did you know?

The introduction of wolves into Yellowstone has allowed grey wolf numbers to increase – up to over 100 in the park, and more than 370 live in the Greater Yellowstone ecosystem.

What was the wider impact of the return of the wolves?

Many plants and animals benefited when the wolves returned to Yellowstone.

The loss of riverside trees and the erosion that this caused had destroyed the habitat needed by beavers and caused beavers to nearly disappear from Yellowstone. The beavers needed the trees near rivers for food and to build dams to survive.

Beaver dams slow the movement of water in rivers and streams and provide sheltered pools for animals to live in. Without the beaver dams, the number of otters and other water animals had declined. With the return of the wolves, beaver numbers increased, as did the number of otters and waterbirds.

With more trees, bird numbers also increased. Bear numbers increased because there was more food for the bears to eat. Perhaps most importantly, the river system became much more stable now that the trees that grew along the banks were able to regenerate.

What has been learned?

Scientists have studied the effects of returning wolves to Yellowstone for more than 20 years now. They have learned that animals that sit at the top of the food chain are vital for the health of ecosystems. They have been surprised by the far-reaching consequences of the wolves for animals and plants that seemed to have no clear relationship to the wolves.

Perhaps the most important lesson has been understanding that every living thing in an ecosystem is important to the health of that ecosystem and that if and when people change things, unforeseen results may occur.

? Did you know?

Yellowstone has played an important role in the survival of the trumpeter swan. In 1930, there were thought to be as few as 63 trumpeter swans in Yellowstone. Today, there are more than 46,000 trumpeter swans in the United States. Yellowstone Lake has been an important habitat in this recovery.

Caring for Yellowstone

Protecting the delicate balance that exists in Yellowstone is the job of rangers. To do their job well, they need to understand how the natural cycles that occur in this amazing ecosystem work. They need to know which plants and animals live there and how these plants and animals relate to each other. They need to manage fires and droughts. And they need to ensure that the things people do don't upset the balance of the ecosystem.

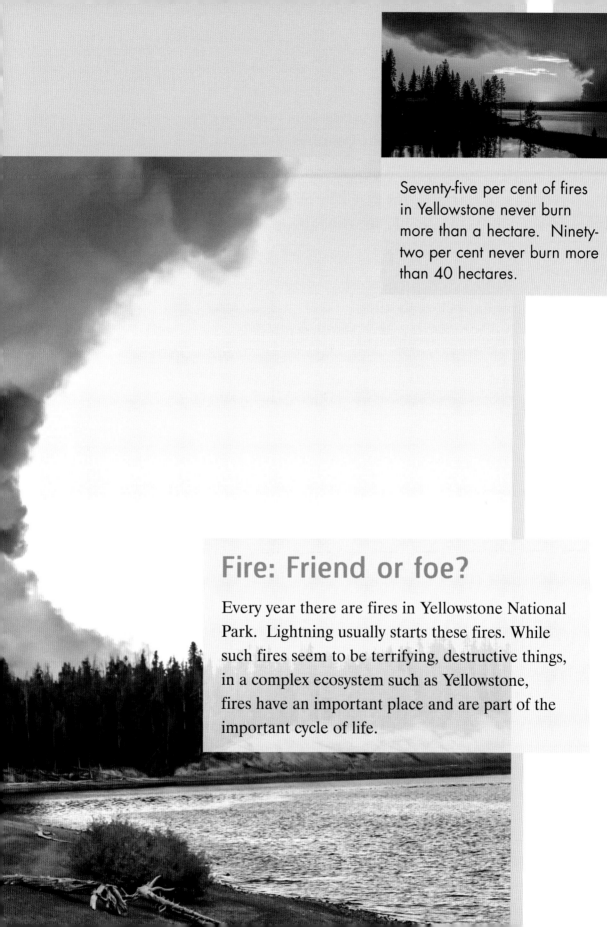

Seventy-five per cent of fires in Yellowstone never burn more than a hectare. Ninety-two per cent never burn more than 40 hectares.

Fire: Friend or foe?

Every year there are fires in Yellowstone National Park. Lightning usually starts these fires. While such fires seem to be terrifying, destructive things, in a complex ecosystem such as Yellowstone, fires have an important place and are part of the important cycle of life.

The benefits of fire

Fires burn leaf litter and old trees, renewing the forest. Many plants rely on fire to reproduce. Fire recycles the **minerals** and other nutrients of the park, making these nutrients available for new plants and animals.

Fire opens up spaces in the forest where new plants can grow. Some plants such as the lodgepole pine need fire to release their seeds. Others need fire to keep stronger plants from taking over an area.

Grasses often grow more strongly after fires. This is because the fire burns away the tops of grasses, but does not damage the root systems, which are under the ground. When the old, dry tops of the grass burn, ash, which is rich in nutrients that grasses need, is deposited on the soil. With more nutrients, the grass grows more quickly and more densely.

After a fire, the plant-eating animals have a lot to eat, such as newly sprouting grass, new leaves emerging from the charred trunks of trees, even burned bark, which is rich in nutrients. The fire also creates hollows in older trees. These hollows are important because they provide nesting holes for birds and animals such as squirrels.

With more lush plant growth, plant-eating animals have more food and can more easily raise their young. Hunting animals then have more opportunity to find food as well.

Lodgepole pine trees

Lodgepole pine trees make up about 80 per cent of the forests in Yellowstone. These trees grow cones filled with pine nuts from which new lodgepole pine trees can grow. These pinecones do not easily open because of a sticky coating of resin that acts like a glue keeping the pinecones shut. During fires, the resin melts, the pinecones open, and the pine nuts are released. Without fires, only a few pine nuts are released.

Fire also provides a good environment for the pine nuts to grow. Mature lodgepole pine forests are filled with tall trees that block out most of the sunlight from the forest floor. This makes it difficult for new plants to begin to grow. Fires kill many of the older trees in the forest and burn away the needles of other pine trees. This opens up spaces and lets sunlight reach the forest floor. The young trees need sunlight to grow. As well, the ash the fire leaves behind returns the minerals and other nutrients the trees had in their leaves and trunks to the ground. This enables the new plants to grow quickly, renewing the forest.

THE NEWS

Bioblitz gives Yellowstone a clean bill of health

August 2016

Last week, about 125 scientists and volunteers conducted a one-day study called a bioblitz to observe and document as many different living things as possible in an approximately five-square-kilometre area of Yellowstone National Park.

This study hoped to collect a snapshot of the biodiversity in the park so that the health of Yellowstone could be measured and used to compare to previous and future data. This is important research as it presents a quick and direct way to determine what effects things like climate change have on the park.

Last week's bioblitz recorded the existence of more than 1,200 species, including a number that had not been seen in Yellowstone before. On this day, 46 kinds of bees, 373 plant species, 86 mushroom types, 5 kinds of bats, 24 butterflies and more than 300 kinds of insects were observed. This huge number of different lifeforms shows that Yellowstone is a healthy ecosystem with a rich biodiversity.

Ann Rodman helped organise the bioblitz. She said that this study, while only a snapshot, was important because it "lets people see that the value of Yellowstone is not just the big mammals we preserve for people to see. There's a whole lot more here."

Rodman also said that while worms, mushrooms and beetles may not be as interesting as the bears, elk and wolves that the park is famous for, they are important. Understanding how they fit into the park is a much-needed addition to knowledge about how to care for and maintain Yellowstone National Park as the amazing ecosystem that so many people love.

Conclusion

Wild places such as Yellowstone have much to contribute to the health of the earth. Scientists have called these places the lungs of the world. In Yellowstone, the huge lodgepole pine forests and sweeping grasslands clean the air and store carbon in their roots and trunks and leaves. This is vital if people are to have clean, breathable air.

Yellowstone must be protected, not only because it is unique and beautiful. It must be protected because the amazing habitats contained within its borders are found nowhere else on Earth. Once they are gone, they cannot be replaced.

Perhaps most importantly, Yellowstone needs to be protected because it is home for many **endangered** animals. Because Yellowstone has been protected for many years, critically endangered animals such as grizzly bears, grey wolves, wolverines and bald eagles are now thriving within the borders of the park.

Yellowstone National Park must continue to be protected. It is a precious place and should be there for people to enjoy for centuries to come.

Glossary

adaptations changes in the way a living thing looks or acts, which help it to survive and reproduce in its habitat

alpine relating to high mountain areas

endangered having a serious risk of becoming extinct

erosion the wearing away of the land by water, wind or ice moving over the land

glaciers slow-moving rivers of ice that form when snow is compacted

interdependence when one group of living things needs other groups of living things for its survival

minerals a solid, non-living substance that occurs naturally in the world

plateau an area of mostly flat ground high up on a mountain

pristine never having been spoiled by human development

regenerate regrowth of a forest or other ecosystem

super-heated when a liquid such as water is heated to a temperature higher than the point at which it boils

temperate a climate that has mostly mild temperatures

thermal vents openings in the earth that allow boiling water or steam to escape into the air.

Index